Wrest

Wrest

POEMS

Hillary Schofield

REVELORE PRESS

*I offer this in gratitude
to all the
guides and nurturers
in my life*

*with
special acknowledgement
to the ways of*
SATURN

♄

Wrest
© Hillary Schofield 2019.

All rights reserved. No part of this publication may be reproduced or utilized in any form or by any means, electronic or mechanical, including photocopying, recording, or by any information storage and retrieval system, without permission in writing from the Publishers.

Book and cover design by Joseph Uccello.
Cover illustration: Hillary Schofield

ISBN: 978-1-947544-24-6

Printed in the United States of America

First printed by Revelore Press in 2019

Revelore Press
220 2nd Ave S #91
Seattle, WA 98104
United States

www.revelore.press

CONTENTS

HOME
9

LINEAGE
11

CONFESS
13

INTRIGUE
15

INTRAVENOUS
17

NOUMENA
19

ENTRANCE
21

REAP
23

TONGUE
25

SNARE
27

SPHINCTER
29

ROPE
31

COMMUNE
33

CONVEYOR
35

RATIO
37

RIPE
39

WREST
41

home

returning
to the
body
was the scariest thing
I have ever done

lineage

if we have given
glimpse
per chance
the fates seize us
with a pain precise
all idol singed
in steadfast tread
we are wrung
the poisons bled
and with exaction
do we breach
a curse
on which
ecstatic traces
mend

confess

a
sustained
monotonous
moan

intrigue

a vague thing extends
to ingest surreptitious
a matter that stirs
its host's diminution

a lump in the gut
assuring its stay
—and who?
has been kept
by this perverse
guest

intravenous

things
are
excruciatingly
pure

noumena

I was heiress to
the ashes
it seemed an obvious
estate
with the dust I fashioned
a body
and fondled at my fate
I flung the thing and
pulled it back—
I watched for signs of sin
and gnawing on the
implications:
the sacrifice—
it hovers in the midst!

it's a natural affair
to grasp the contours of
our skin—and then
with shudder/strange release
a vast expanse:
arousal
indefinite

entrance

through
contrast
the carnival
is erected

reap

I was plucked
and cast as dead
in the thicket of
sovereign neglect
but in the damp
and in decay
I have in sympathy
grown veins

*jagged peaks
of bone at tide
skin like water
tattered sheath*

it is time that
we came in
—they tell me she
is full now...though
in the
blindness of
their bane

tongue

putting pressure
on the joints
stimulates our
reciprocity

lineage/genesis

as they flinch
we flinch
and resonate with
enmeshed
deliverance

snare

an intermediate
a by-way
a chance

under the specter of
hypocrisy
I swallow stirred
weakness

it is not they who bind
my faults in being
what?
a witness

where the wood is rot
a snap
and stays
no further prospect

sphincter

when my flesh recedes
my bones be given
unto compass
five points toward infinity
and where they meet
divine orifice
all is hole, we float

rope

it's your teat
and you will
milk it
and in turn
you are
secreted

commune

hand pressed
to glass
in honor of
water
fingers
convinced
through
transference
through heat
I am a mound
where the
elements
decipher quiet
and spread
meandering
truss

conveyor

it is as a clamp that
comes down
and this is the shape
you see
the brain, extruded
wet clay through
fist splay
this is the shape
you see
a body or
such limbs
thought wrung
in sequence

ratio

to be slow
is to be
close

ripe

I hold my spine
just below the ribs

I see its contours now

so cleverly disguised
anyone would think it was
of me, anyone
including I

for long I've sensed
something amiss
something not
quite right
yet it's hard to risk
the felling of a thing
vouched as it were
with essence!

when my sap has
been convinced
and feeds it life
no further
—a familiar
strangeness
drops then from an
unsuspecting other

wrest

this
is for
the delicate
thread
of vigilance
excruciatingly
shorn
unverifiable
only felt
only worth
repletion

Wrest *was typeset in SangBleu,*
designed by Ian Party/Swiss Typefaces.

www.ingramcontent.com/pod-product-compliance
Lightning Source LLC
Chambersburg PA
CBHW052107110526
44591CB00013B/2386